PAINTING
SEASCAPES
A CREATIVE APPROACH

PAINTING SEASCAPES
A CREATIVE APPROACH

BY JOHN RAYNES

WATSON-GUPTILL PUBLICATIONS/NEW YORK

First published in the United States of America 1972 by Watson-Guptill Publications,
a division of Billboard Publications, Inc.,
165 West 46 Street, New York, N.Y.

Copyright© 1971 by John Raynes
First published 1971 in Great Britain by Studio Vista Limited,
Blue Star House, Highgate Hill, London N19

Manufactured in Japan

First Printing, 1972

Library of Congress Cataloging in Publication Data

Raynes, John, 1929-
  Painting seascapes.

  Bibliography: p.
  1. Marine painting—Technique. I. Title.
ND1370.R3   751   76-190515
ISBN 0-8230-3855-6

Contents

Introduction, 7

1. Equipment and Materials, 9

Choosing Your Medium, 9
Packing Your Paint Kit, 9
Advantages of Carrying Frames, 19
Easels, 19

2. The Color of the Sea, 21

Color Theory, 21
Pigments, 21
Primary and Complementary Colors, 21
Color Key in Painting, 26
Laying Out Your Palette, 26
Mixing and Matching Colors, 28
Making Color Sketches of the Sea, 29
Color Changes of the Sea, 33
Using Photos, 33
Pointillism, 33

3. The Shape of the Sea, 35

Placing the Horizon Line, 35
Compositional Devices, 36
Tonal Values, 37
Patterns, 45
Perspective, 45

4. The Mobile Sea, 47

Studying the Moving Sea, 47
Studying Waves, 47
Taking Notes and Making Sketches, 56
Wave Patterns, 56

Making a "Statement," 56
A Few Pitfalls to Avoid, 59
Some Great Sea Paintings, 59

5. The Shore, 61

Studying Shoreline Rocks, 61
Using Your Imagination, 61
Monoprinting, 63
Many Facets of Seascapes, 63
Painting Outdoors versus Comfort, 69
Searching for the Right View, 70
Other Objects in Composition, 80

6. Flora and Fauna, 85

Shells, 85
Crustaceans, 85
Seaweed, 85
Subaquatic Views, 85
Fish, 88
Painting from Our Own Sea Experiences, 88

7. Man and the Sea, 93

Boats, 93
Seaside Structures, 93
Seaside Patterns and Colors, 93
Selective Vision, 95
Interpretive Painting, 101

Conclusion, 113

Bibliography, 115

Index, 117

Introduction

Painting seascapes is unusually demanding and challenging because the sea moves and changes color with great speed and variety. Water reflects the changing sky and interacts with it in a much more immediate way than do most landscapes.

The sea's form is never constant: it can assume the appearance of a plain or of a mountain range; and it is rarely still enough to be observed and drawn objectively, in the way that we can deal with land forms. The continuous impact of the mobile sea on the rigid land edge produces diverse shorelines, which are changing and evolving much more rapidly than inland earth contours. It is here at the sea shore that the most rapid laying bare of geological history is occurring. Most of us live on the soil or road-covered surface of the land, and only where rivers or glaciers or the sea have made an incision do we see what underlies the benign slopes. Cliff strata give evidence of cataclysmic forces and pressures, which often belie the relatively calm forms sloping to them. For me, this revelation of natural forces gives to seascapes and shorescapes an immediate and elemental quality rarely found inland. Most people, at some time, feel a sense of awe at the sight and sound of the ocean, even from the safety of the shore, and the huge blocks of stone dumped onto promenades after spring gales can leave no doubt about the ocean's power.

I realize, of course, that the sea can also mean a gentle lapping on soft sand, and paddling and sand castles and ice cream; and that this is an aspect which is just as valid, just as expressible in painting as the more robust moods. However, I believe that the more we have to do with the sea, the more respectful of its latent power we become, and that if the essence of the sea is searched for in the shapes of the stones and rocks, the shales, even the sands that are formed by it; in the structure of boats designed to sail on it; and of anchors and anchor chains and breakwaters and jetties, we are inescapably led to an idea of awesome power rather than prettiness.

Therefore, I do not intend in this book to talk much about the seaside as a resort, fascinating though this may be in its own way, but to suggest that you try to discover that essence of the sea which is independent of humanity. The sea was here long before us, and will doubtless still be here when we are gone. It is this total immunity from man's control (except for a few dykes and sea walls that are soon destroyed unless they are constantly renewed) that I find fascinating and would like, if only I could, to express in drawings and paintings. It is comparatively easy to talk about, quite a lot more difficult to put down in paint, but there are clues and certain practical procedures which simplify the activity and make it possible to concentrate fully on the meaning without too much struggle with the method. It is in these aspects that I will try to help.

Polperro, Cornwall. This felt-pen sketch, done on illustration board, was an exercise in recording notes from observation of seaside locales.

CHAPTER ONE

Equipment and materials

When I talk about the equipment necessary for the special subject of seascape painting, the assumption will be that a great deal of work is to be undertaken outdoors, some way off the beaten track, and quite possibly in arduous and exposed conditions.

Apart from the unique requirements of such possible conditions, the equipment will be much the same as for any other outdoor painting.

Figure 3 is a diagram in which I have tried to summarize the minimum recommended requirements for paints, brushes, media, and surfaces in the three media mainly used—oils, watercolors, and acrylics. Below is a suggested list for preparing a reduced kit for drawing.

(1) Inks: waterproof black, brown, yellow
(2) Paints: acrylic black, acrylic opaque white, gouache jet black, flake white (transparent), raw sienna
(3) Brushes, black felt-tipped pens, pencils in various grades, two pens—fine and broad
(4) Surfaces and palette
(5) Water bottle and jar

Surfaces and palette clipped together, everything else in duffel bag.

I have included a small range of waterproof colored inks in this latter, but they could equally well be included with watercolors or even acrylics, although they do not always mix too well with acrylic mediums and are normally repelled by the plastic paint. They do serve very well as an underpainting though, and acrylics can be used over them without problems.

Choosing Your Medium

The choice of media for seascape painting is a personal one, of course, but it does seem to me more sensible and convenient to use water-based paints for general use outdoors. Water is easier to carry and, of course, to replenish; the paints dry quickly to allow underpainting and overpainting several times in a day's painting. And the paintings are easy to carry home. Cleaning up brushes, palette (and self) is rather easier too, and in my experience an oil kit is usually rather heavier to carry, although I suppose this is not necessarily always so. Acrylic paints can be used in a similar way to oil paints anyway, and it is difficult or impossible to tell the difference in a completed painting.

Two points in favor of oils on location: first, the very fact that they dry slowly can be useful if you like to move the paint about and paint wet-in-wet, or for hot conditions, when the drying of acrylics is accelerated so much that they solidify on the palette before you have had a chance to use them; and second, they can be used in the rain. This may seem a doubtful advantage, but sometimes you are subjected to a gentle shower or just a few drops of rain or sea spray—not enough to have to shelter yourself, but very damaging to a water-based painting—even acrylics which dry quickly can be affected to a limited extent, only the very freshly applied paint being vulnerable. It does happen, rarely and luckily, that rain drops on a watercolor drawing produce an exciting improvement, but this cannot be relied on!

Indoors in the studio, when weight and drying time are not such vital factors, the choice of paints is even more a matter of personal taste, and at some time, perhaps, all should be experimented with—not all in one painting, I might add. Although this is possible, there is no special advantage in mixing media to this extent, and the problems involved are unnecessary.

My advice, therefore, is to keep your medium simple.

1. Study of a Calm Sea. To capture the essence of the sea in its different movements is no easy task. But in studies such as this one of a calm sea, reflected sky tones and the shape of the water were easily painted with gouache on illustration board.

2. Calm Day at Lyme Regis, Dorset. This pen and ink sketch shows one of the innumerable ways to portray the sea—framed by harbors, boathouses, piers, and boats.

	COLORS	MEDIUMS	BRUSHES	SURFACES
OIL PAINTS	Permanent rose (Quinacridone) Cadmium red or less expensive equivalent Cadmium orange or less expensive equivalent Aureolin or azo yellow Lemon yellow or Hansa yellow Winsor emerald Winsor green (phthalocyanine) Cerulean blue Ultramarine blue Winsor blue (phthalocyanine) Winsor violet or dioxazine purple Raw sienna Raw umber Burnt umber Ivory black or Mars black Flake white Titanium white	Turpentine Linseed oil	1 in. bristle house-painting brush No. 10 Filbert bristle, long No. 12 flat bristle No. 8 (two of these) Filbert bristle ⅜ in. flat oxhair and sable No. 4 round sable No. 2 round sable	Canvas Primed board or wood panel Canvas-textured paper
WATERCOLORS	Permanent rose (quinacridone) Scarlet lake or cadmium red Cadmium orange Gamboge or cadmium yellow Winsor green Cerulean blue French ultramarine (blue) Winsor blue (phthalocyanine) Permanent mauve or Winsor violet Payne's gray or neutral tint Raw sienna Burnt umber Blue black Cadmium yellow, permanent yellow or azo yellow Permanent rose (quinacridone) Cadmium red or naphthol red Cadmium orange	Water	1 in. flat or No. 10 round: squirrel hair wash brush ½ in. flat pure sable ⅛ in. flat pure sable No. 6 round sable No. 3 round sable	Handmade paper, rough or smooth surface, mounted on board or stretched
ACRYLICS	Lemon yellow or Hansa yellow light Yellow green (called by a great variety of names) Winsor or monastral green (phthalocyanine) Peacock blue or turquoise Ultramarine blue Winsor or monastral blue (phthalocyanine) Spectrum violet or dioxazine purple Raw sienna Burnt sienna Raw umber Permanent white (titanium, opaque) Flake white (relatively transparent) Ivory black or Mars black	Water Acrylic mediums, gloss and/or matt	1 in. flat oxhair ⅜ in. flat oxhair and sable 3/16 in. flat sable ⅛ in. flat sable No. 2 round sable No. 4 round sable	Smooth-coated paper, mounted on board Handmade paper, smooth or rough Primed hardboard, canvas or almost anything

3. (Left) This chart lists the suggested minimum equipment necessary for painting seascapes in different media: paints, brushes, mediums, and surfaces.

4. (Right) Your paint equipment can be put into three basic packages—paintbox; palette, painting surfaces, easel; and duffel bag—all of which can be strapped to a carrying frame.

5. A toolbox or fisherman's tackle box like this one is ideal for holding tubes of paint, mediums, painting knives, brushes, etc.

Packing Your Paint Kit

I have also included a suggested list for packing your full-color paint kit:

(1) Paintbox: paints, mediums, brushes, palette knife, pencils, pens, ink, mat knife, razor blades, rag, sponge, sticking tape, canvas tacks and thumbtacks

(2) Painting surfaces: various, clipped together

(3) Palette

(4) Water or turpentine: for replenishing water jar or dipper

(5) Portable easel with water jar attached

(6) Carrying frame

(7) Duffel bag: camera, drinking water, food, spare pullover, and anorak (parka or windbreaker)

When you have decided whether oil-based or water-based paints suit you best, it is as well, I think, to equip yourself comprehensively with one or the other, rather than with dribs and drabs of both. This applies especially to the outdoor kit, where compactness and complete self-sufficiency are essential. The type of painting case I find to be most useful is one with compartments into which I can drop groups of colors—i.e., one box for yellows, one for blues, etc.—good deep compartments into which tubes can be dropped or thrown, not requiring careful placing. Manufactured paintboxes, displaying tubes of paint arranged in a long neat row, I view with little enthusiasm. What happens when the tubes are partly used and folded up? They do not sit in their neat little molded depressions any more, but lie about in unidentified heaps. Colors take vital irritating extra seconds to find, and such small deterrents as these are often enough to persuade you almost unconsciously to use a color already out on the palette instead of finding and squeezing out new clean color.

Just recently, I saw a box which a student

6. Here are the suggested materials for working in black and white: a mat knife, pens, bottles of ink, tubes of color, palette knife, and brushes.

7. This is the ideal, simple outdoor paint kit: paint-box, duffel bag, and palette and painting surfaces clipped to the easel. All this is strapped with elastic onto a carrying frame.

had discovered in a sports shop, surprisingly, which was adapted splendidly for use as a paint and materials case. Its designed use was as a fisherman's tackle box—for hooks, flies and whatnot—and I have drawn it in Figure 5. Although the compartments are not as deep as I would like, the three trays plus the deep box at the bottom allow for a good deal of easily maintained separation of color groups, and everything is very easily and immediately available. This, of course, is the whole point—the painting is the important thing; what goes down there is what matters, and the less time and attention given to the mechanics of painting, the more attention can be focused on the painting itself. Good equipment will not ensure a good painting, but inaccessible or incomplete equipment militates against producing a painting at all.

The basic painting case, in addition to paints in color groups if possible, should have room for water or turpentine/oil container, and for brushes, palette knife, mediums, canvas tacks (if oils are used—for keeping wet paintings apart), rag, and various useful odds and ends such as razor blades, mat knife, sticky tape, thumbtacks. Bulk water or turpentine supply is usually better carried separately. I use a small duffel bag for this, and for camera, drinking water, food, spare pullover, and anorak (parka). Painting surfaces and palette can be clipped together, and a lightweight folding easel completes the equipment. A folding stool is very useful, but I do without one, and usually manage to find a reasonably comfortable perch. It could be argued that a stool is more useful than an easel for seascape painting, as the winds on cliff tops and sea fronts are often too severe for any

8. (Right) Sketching outdoors may prove to be a problem because moisture and sea spray could wet the inks. Be prepared to accept inclement weather too.

9. There are three types of easels which serve different purposes: (A) is a radial easel and holds paintings about 30″ x 40″; (B) holds paintings approximately 20″ x 30″; and (C) is a studio easel which holds paintings wider than 40″.

A

B

C

folding easel to withstand. In gale force winds, I have had to hang onto my drawing board as hard as I could with *both* hands to avoid its being torn from my grip by sudden gusts, only releasing one hand to paint with in the lulls between. I have never tried it, but perhaps some sort of strap fastening the board to your knees might be useful in trying conditions—a comic image, but if it is effective, who cares?

Rain and spray can also make sea painting a problem, but if you really want to learn about the sea, you have to be prepared to get a little wet. It is essential to realize that conditions by the sea can change rapidly and to be equipped for the worst. Even on a hot summer day, it is worth taking a wind and waterproof anorak or similar garment, and at any other time of the year a thick sweater, too. Sitting for two or three hours in even a light sea breeze dissipates body heat surprisingly effectively!

Advantages of Carrying Frames

Having collected the equipment into three basic packages—paintbox; surfaces, palette, easel; and duffel bag for everything else—you should then put the whole lot on a carrying frame. I use one as illustrated in Figure 7, and fix everything to it with elastic straps. Although the paintbox alone weighs 20 lbs., once on my back the whole lot is quite easy to carry, and it is no problem to walk a few miles, and clamber over rocky or stony beaches.

With the reduced kit (using only monochrome), the carrying frame is so lightly laden that it can almost be disregarded, and it is possible to negotiate quite rocky foreshores or even steep cliffs, if you are a better climber than I am.

It is not only that weight is easier to carry on your back, it is equally important that it leaves your hands free, making rock clambering very much easier and safer.

I have also used the unloaded carrying frame as an improvised seat on rough surfaces, so altogether I consider it to be a worthwhile, even essential, part of outdoor painting equipment.

Easels

Indoors, the only additional equipment needed is a more substantial easel. Sketching easels will do, but are not ideal, especially if you intend to work on rather larger paintings. Most lightweight easels will not hold a painting rigidly over a size of about 20″ by 15″. A radial easel (Figure 9A) is fine for up to about 30″ by 40″, if the surface itself is rigid. Larger paintings, if they are higher than they are wide, can be held satisfactorily, but if much wider than 40″, they really need a studio easel (Figure 9C). Some painters can use two radials side by side for very wide paintings (Figure 10).

10. This easel with two radials side by side is used for very wide paintings.

CHAPTER TWO

The color of the sea

Sea and sky, to people who do not often look, are always blue. The truth is that only if the sky is blue will the sea be blue also. The two are interdependent; the sea is a great mirror of the sky, and is constantly changing as the sky changes. It can be almost any color, in fact, but is most often seen in the green-blue hue range.

Color Theory

To explain what is meant by "hue" and to discuss color further, it is first necessary to talk about color theory a little.

The components of sunlight can be split into the visible range known as the spectrum. Although these components are usually named as red, orange, yellow, green, blue, indigo, violet, it is really an infinitely subtle gradation through all these colors. One thing they all have in common is that they are pure and unadulterated by black or white; there are no grays, browns, pinks, or ochres. When I use the term "hue" I mean it to refer to a point in this pure spectral range.

A color which is not in itself of the spectrum can be described, and indeed mixed, by identifying its basic hue and then adding white to adjust the concentration of hue, and black to adjust the tone. To mix by this method successfully, it is obviously necessary to get the hue *exactly* right, and although it is not possible to have paints representing every infinitely subtle gradation of the spectrum, we can choose a range from which they can be mixed.

Pigments

Pigments are not colors in themselves; they are substances which have a particular color, and which retain that color when mixed with a vehicle or medium—such as oil, gum, or acrylic—which allows us to apply them as paint on various surfaces.

Many of these substances are not a bit like spectral colors—the earliest and still some of the most permanent pigments were the earth colors made from colored clays, mostly in the yellow-brown range. Luckily though, pigments such as carmine (cochineal), vermilion (mercuric sulfide), ultramarine (lapis lazuli), chrome yellow (lead chromate) are nearer to colors of the spectrum, and theoretically it should be possible to mix any hue, using only red, yellow, and blue. In practice, unless these three primaries are very carefully chosen and very pure, it is not possible to mix the whole spectrum.

Primary and Complementary Colors

In modern color printing, the use of a combination of magenta (a pink-red completely devoid of orange), cyan (a slightly greenish blue), and process yellow (pure, strong mid-yellow), plus black makes a pretty good job of imitating all the colors of nature. For painters, it is easier to supplement these three primaries with hues midway between them, i.e., a clear mid-orange (between red and yellow), a strong green (between blue and yellow), and a violet (between red and blue).

These colors are called secondaries, as they are theoretically obtainable from mixing the primaries, and they are placed in a color circle between their component primaries and opposite the third primary (Figure 12). The color circle, you will realize, is just a simplified spectrum bent round on itself, the purple (which is not of the spectrum) being added to join violet and red together and complete the circle. Colors opposite each other in the color circle are called complementaries; thus yellow is complementary to violet, green to red, and blue to orange. A fact that is often over

11. Sea Sketch. The color of the sea can be noted in pen and ink on paper. Variations in tone can be indicated in monochrome.

12. The circle of the color spectrum shows the primary and secondary colors. Colors opposite each other are called "complementaries." Any straight line such as A to B will link complementaries.

Sunlight ▼

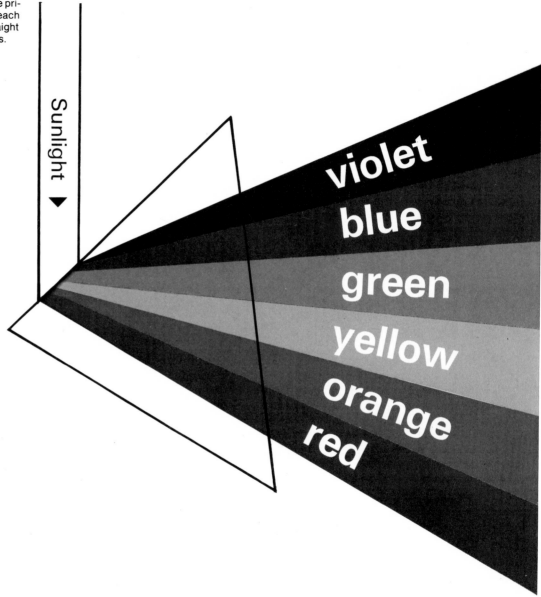

violet

blue

green

yellow

orange

red

Non-Spectral Purple

14.(Above) **Boat in Harbour, Brittany** by Christopher Wood. The artist's interpretation of form and perspective gives this painting its charm and simplicity. (The Tate Gallery, London)

13. (Left) **Seascape** by Nicholas de Stael. The simplicity of this painting belies the artist's earnest observation of the marine atmosphere. A central color key was chosen which gives the painting its strength. (Private Collection. Photo Arts Council of Great Britain and Courtauld Institute of Art) looked is that this holds true for all the intermediate hues, too. Any straight line through the center of the color circle will link complementary pairs; the line AB links a yellow-orange with a cold blue, say ultramarine. Complementary pairs of colors are very useful, because they have the peculiar quality of reacting with each other if placed close together and causing a little vibration to occur between them, sometimes only mildly registering as a strong color contrast, but with some colors—notably reds and greens—producing violently dazzling effects. Painters began to see this phenomenon consciously only fairly recently, from the late nineteenth century in France, when much experimenting with the science of color was being pursued. If you are interested in these aspects, look at the work of the French impressionists, the pointillists especially and the fauves—a French post-impressionist movement—and also the work of Paul Gauguin. He was not a marine painter but he made great use of the tension between complementary hues in his color compositions. So also do the Op Art painters, who set out to disturb and deceive the eye, to create movement, to dazzle or even to produce nausea, simply from the juxtaposition of abstract shapes and color.

Color Key in Painting

I have chosen the colors listed in Figure 3 by balancing the ease of obtaining any color you wish by minimum mixing against the expense and encumbrance of too massive a collection. You *could* work with less, but I think it would be unnecessarily restricting. I personally keep a vast range of colors in various types of paint, so that I can choose a working range with a bias toward a certain color key. By color key I mean a sort of "home" color or group of colors, which I start off with when doing a color composition. Although many other colors

flaming-hot red, while a small amount of blue transforms it into a cold violet or purple. I treat such a pure pink-red as a useful link between hot and cold. All colors which are admixtures of cool colors will be cool also; and similarly, warm colors mixed together never go cool. Add to this the fact that adjacent hues in the spectral range harmonize with each other, and when mixed together produce a very clean intermediate hue, and it becomes apparent that a palette layout based on spectral order and color temperature will make for cleanest mixtures and greatest order.

Figure 15 shows the two palette layouts employing these principles. The cool layout differs only from the warm one by virtue of the extension of the blue-green range of colors in the cool layout, as against the orange-red extension in the other. Browns, ochres, and siennas *can* be mixed by addition of black with spectral hues, but most people prefer to include them in the working range. I think it is a good idea; they are beautiful colors, especially raw umber and sienna, and it takes a lot of fiddling about to mix them satisfactorily. Their position on the palette in this system is slightly tricky, but I usually place ochre and siennas with the warm yellow-oranges, and the browns somewhere close to black. Even if your intention is only to use a very limited range of color, the palette order should be so habitual that the paints are still placed in their full-palette layout positions.

If colors are mixed on spaces on the palette somewhere between the mixed colors or adjacent to one of them, the mixing areas tend to adjust themselves into four groups. Close to white on the cool side will be an area of cool tints, and on the other side, warm tints will predominate. Near to black will be cool blue and purple shades, and warm red and orange shades. (Tints are hues to which white has been added;

may be introduced, they are chosen in relation to the "key" either by harmonizing with it or consciously kicking against it. I think it is important to have a positive color idea of this sort. Otherwise, the painting becomes either entirely descriptive and a slavish imitation of what is seen, which will probably not really be as it is (and a camera does it better anyway); or, while striving for a personal interpretation, we tend to use too many color ideas and the painting becomes disorganized and fragmented. Too many colors, too many ideas, without any feeling of complete "oneness" is a very common fault. It is really best to keep the elements of a picture simple and working together, adding more complications if you wish as your organizational competence increases. For myself, I prefer the simple solutions anyway. Look at the Nicholas de Stael (Figure 13) and the Christopher Wood (Figure 14)— such simplicity, but the very essence of marine atmosphere.

Laying Out Your Palette

A great help in keeping the color of a painting under control is a system of palette layout. Certain colors (such as orange and orange-reds) are thought of as warm colors, and blues and blue-greens are fairly obviously cool. In fact, it becomes quite useful to divide all colors into warm or cool categories. Thus violet, through purplish blues, ultramarine, green-blues, blue-greens, mid-green, yellow-greens, and perhaps greenish yellow constitute the cool to cold category; and mid-yellow through orange-yellow, yellow-orange, orange, orange-reds to bright reds, are in the warm to hot category. This classification leaves the pure magenta red in a slightly ambiguous position—it is a very cool red, but *as* a red it belongs in the hot category! The slightest amount of yellow added, and it is a

15. Here are the suggested layouts for a warm palette and a cool palette. The adjacent hues that harmonize with one another when mixed will produce a clean intermediate hue.

Mixing Colors

Black plus a little cadmium yellow	= dark olive green
Cadmium yellow plus a spot of black	= lime green
Viridian plus raw sienna	= light olive green
Viridian plus a little orange	= mid-olive green
Viridian plus a little cadmium red	= rich dark green
Burnt umber plus lemon yellow	= raw sienna
Orange plus a little viridian	= variant of raw sienna
Cadmium red plus a spot of viridian	= rich mid-brown
Cadimum red plus ultramarine	= inky mauve
Ultramarine (blue) plus a little orange lake	= brownish purple
Ultramarine (blue) plus orange lake	= mid-warm brown

16. The table above shows colors which can be mixed for various hues. It is good exercise to mix a color, and then to attempt to match the color mixed.

shades are hues with black admixed.) The mixings will not remain this orderly for long; as the space is used up, mixings tend to roam all over the palette. When it gets so crowded that accidental bleeding over from adjacent mixings occurs, or if it becomes necessary to mix over other dry or semi-dry paint, then it is time to stop, clean off the palette, and start fresh.

You may think that I am stressing this matter of palette order unduly, and that such orderliness would be inhibiting. The contrary is true, I·believe; although it takes some time to describe the procedure, it takes no less time to place colors haphazardly than to put them down in a habitual order, and the habit of mixing clean intentional colors, once formed, actually saves time and leaves you freer to think about the painting itself.

Mixing and Matching Colors

Now that you have a good complement of colors laid out in order on the palette, it might be well to list some of the possible mixtures available by direct admixture of two pigments. I am often asked, even by art students (who should know better), how to match colors, and it is worth taking a little time experimentally mixing colors together in varying proportions, noting the result and then perhaps trying to match it by choosing a hue and adding black and/or white. You will soon develop the ability to look at an admixture and say what needs to be added to it to match a required final result. As a general guide, Figure 16 shows a short selection from the infinity of possibilities.

Of course, there is a great deal more that can be theorized about color and color mixing, and if you are interested to pursue the subject further, there is a book in this series devoted to the subject, *Colour for the Artist* by Hans Schwartz.

Making Color Sketches of the Sea

Just as important as being able to put down the color intended is the ability to make decisions about the color of the world about us. To return to the subject with which I began this chapter, the color of the sea, there is no one answer to this. Observation is the thing; *really* looking I mean, without preconception. While observing, make notes (color sketches if possible, but otherwise a drawing with written notes) as I did (Figure 17) to record color sensations: Look carefully at the way the sea color changes from foreground to horizon—are the changes due to variations in clarity of the water or are they alternate bands of sunlight and cloud shadow? Is the sea darker of lighter than the sky at the horizon, or exactly the same? When you make color notes of sky and sea, where everything is on the move and changing from one moment to the next, it is probably easiest to do quite small—almost thumbnail—sketches. It is not necessary to completely cover the surface either—a dab of carefully chosen color can be used to denote the color of a complete area. The definition of the limits of the area can be made after the color has been noted, or even later, as it changes. Think of the exercise as the gathering of information rather than the creation of a work of art, so that it does not matter what it looks like as long as it contains genuine discoveries that can be put to use at greater leisure. I often find such fragmentary note-taking studies more exciting to look at than a finished, considered painting, but you should not depend on this or even think about it really Once I start making sketches pretty, I find they degenerate into clichés and shut out any real discovery.

I find that watercolor is the easiest medium for quick note-taking. Open pans in a compact box with the normal folding flaps for mixing on are better than tubes. It is easy and quick to handle, needs the minimum of

17. Making on-the-spot sketches with color notations of seaside scenes is good practice in observation and useful for later work in the studio.

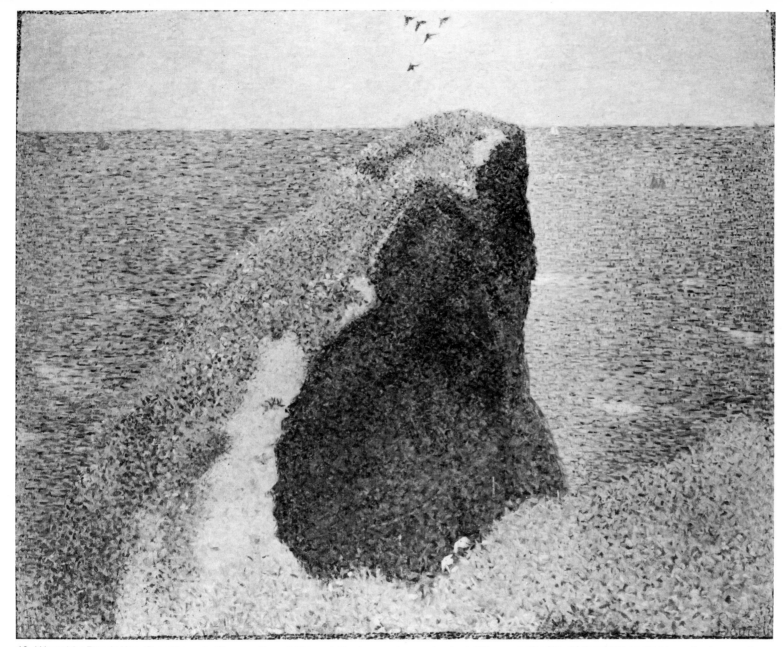

19. (Above) **Le Bec de Hoc, Grandcamp** by Georges Seurat. This painting is a good example of pointillism, a method in which paint is applied in spots of pure color and they seem to merge when the work is observed from a distance. Note how the light sea contrasts with the dark cliff face. (The Tate Gallery, London)

18. (Left) **Sunset.** This wash drawing shows the different tones obtainable in different lights during the day.

20. The tonal steps show each gray is absolutely flat, yet they gradate from left to right as the eye adapts to the different light level.

arrangement and carrying of equipment. If really rapid working is essential and drying time of each wash is a problem, either use the running of washes into each other so that the whole thing is fluid and moving (which is not easy, and requires some experience), or use absorbent paper—heavy handmade watercolor paper or even blotting paper. The washes, if not too full bodied, will dry very quickly to allow other washes to be overlaid. Of course, dabs of color inside defined areas also gets over the problems neatly.

Color Changes of the Sea

The color the sea varies not only with season and weather, but also with the time of day. If it is possible, if you are enthusiastic enough, try visiting the seashore at dawn. Be prepared to go more than once until you catch the sun rising in a clear sky. Watch the color changes at sunset too, and walk along the shore at night (Figure 18). The sea seems very different, much more awesome, at night—when color is at a minimum.

Although direct painting at night is virtually impossible, a moonlit sea leaves a strong impression and may emerge in a painting later.

Using Photos

Many amateur painters like to produce paintings from picture postcards or their own holiday pictures. It is very easy to sneer at this practice, and it does bristle with traps for the unwary, I think. The trouble is that the reality has already been processed; the color film has frozen a certain interpretation of the visual aspects and left out all other sensations—temperature, wind, smell, etc. I am not criticizing the photograph that it does this; it is almost impossible for it not to, but you need to be able to react to these things to make your own interpretation. If

the subject of the photograph is a seascape that you know well and have drawn and made notes about on the spot, then I do not think it a bad thing to take information from it. But it is pointless to try to reproduce the photograph exactly. Extract what you need to supplement your notes, then put it aside and draw on the memory of your feelings about the place. This applies especially to color; photographic color tends to be selective, in that a choice has to be made in exposure between rendering light areas satisfactorily or finding shadow color and detail, and at the same time it is relatively literal and non-interpretive.

Photographers will leap to defend the art form, pointing out that there is a vast amount of choice in the way of filtering, exposure control, printing, double exposure, etc., which allows entirely personal emotive statements. My point is that this is exactly what the painter has to do with the basic information, but with the particular capabilities of the medium and in his own way. The straight photograph is the basic information in each case—the interpretations will probably be very different.

Choosing any picture postcard which appeals and attempting to copy it on a larger scale I don't think a good idea on the whole. I am hesitant to condemn any method of working, and am generally against any prohibitive system of things which are "not done" or thought to be cheating. The result is all important; how it was reached is irrelevant. Nevertheless, I cannot see very much point in reproducing a photographer's work in paint, except perhaps as a technical exercise, and if that, why not use a great painting as a model instead, thereby learning something of a master's method?

Pointillism

Mention of the masters gives me an opportunity to introduce a reproduction of a ma-

rine painting by George Seurat, the famous French pointillist (Figure 19). Pointillism was a method explored by a school of nineteenth-century French painters, in which paint was applied in spots of dabs of varied pure color which, when viewed from a suitable distance, merged into mixtures of those colors. Thus an area which had mainly blue and yellow dots appeared green, pink and pale blue appeared pale violet and so on. The point was that the pigments were not actually mixed; the mixing was effected by the eye, resulting in greater brilliance and iridescence. The pointillists were after an impression of "real" air and light and, indeed, they were an extension of the impressionist school.

Although you will have to look at a pointillist painting yourself to see this color phenomenon at work, Seurat's painting has one or two interesting features even in black and white. Notice how light the sea is where the dark cliff cuts it. The visual illusion it records is the apparent intensifying of tonal change at the *edge division* between contrasting tones, i.e., the dark appears to become darker and the light lighter just where the two meet. It is a very common effect and has something to do with the adaptation of the eye to different light levels, I believe. The tonal steps in Figure 20 show it fairly clearly—each gray is absolutely flat and even in tone, but each appears to gradate left to right.

Seurat has seen that one side of the jutting rock is *light* against the darker sea and the other side is *dark* against light, and has made a feature of it. Compositionally the group of flying birds, the breaking of the horizon by the top of the rock, and the placing of the white sail near to this break are all carefully contrived to give point and center to what is basically a very simple composition and what could have been very boring.

CHAPTER THREE

The shape
of the sea

For the marine painter, composition can be something of a problem. The horizon is nearly always straight, or more accurately such a flattened arc as to appear straight. I say "nearly always" because there are exceptions. A very low viewpoint may allow a breaking wave in the foreground to become the effective skyline, which can then have as much variety as a mountain range. Only the combination of a very low eye level and heavy seas would bring this about in reality, but there is no reason why you should not imagine it and create a swimmer's eye view from the trough of a wave. The woodcut by Hokusai (Figure 35, p. 54) is an example of this type of composition, and of the fanciful symbolic imagery of the East, which, while being unreal in the literal sense, is very powerful and frightening and true in essence. I will talk further about this picture later on, but first of all I should like to consider composition generally.

Placing the Horizon Line

From the most likely beach and cliff viewpoints, looking straight out to sea is going to produce a basic composition which can only be varied by moving the horizon line up or down in the picture. There will always be this pervasive horizontal division. Such compositions can hardly fail, but they are liable to become a little boring. They can be made more interesting by making the most of any pattern that can be found above or below the horizon.

For example, a low eye-level composition would be fine to feature a dramatic cloud formation (Figure 22). Middleground pattern below a sea horizon is used in the sketch in Color Plate 9. The breaking waves bunch the sea activity into an eye-holding nucleus, while the nearer shallow, flowing water on the sand makes an irregular pattern sliding up from one corner and diver-

sifying in its lightest tonal area. Near the middle of that bright area are two little figures walking along the beach, thereby providing a visual center for the picture and, incidentally, giving scale to it. They do look remarkably small, but that is the size they seemed to be; the waves must have been quite large. We often find this to be so; waves seen from the road approaching the bay always look like little ripples until we relate them to the tiny specks on the beach which are people. When we are struggling out on a surfboard, those same waves seem like mountainous roaring monsters determined to hurl us back to the beach.

It is probably not a good idea to place the horizon line exactly halfway up the picture area, unless there is a very good reason for it. An intention to show the extreme symmetry of the view—or the great similarity of sea and sky—could be considered good reason as long as it is really clear that it *was* really intended. Placing an incident-free horizon either above or below the center tends to direct the view generally to the larger section, a movement which can be countered by strong contrast or incident in the smaller part, thereby creating surprise or excitement.

In the painting in Color Plate 1, the horizon line has actually been reinforced by the line of the top of the rock. It is often stated as a law that such confluences must be avoided, but as with most prohibitions they can be made to work for you. In this case, it seemed important *not* to break the calm horizontal, but to use it as a sort of clothesline from which to hang the rest of the composition. In other words, as before, I used the lack of incident at the horizon to direct attention either above or below it.

All the action was occurring at the foot of the cliff, and in actuality the movement was reinforced by sound. The painter—without the assistance of sound or movement—

21. Trebarwith Sands. The composition of cliff, beach, land, and sea helps to vary the skyline in this watercolor sketch.

22. A low eye-level composition can dramatize a cloud formation as shown in this pen and ink sketch. (From seascape by Emile Nolde)

must direct attention by compositional means. Placing the incident area at just the right point of tension between the larger more ponderous shapes is part of it, and leading the eye by convergent lines to the visual center is another useful device.

Compositional Devices

Look at the diagrams (Figure 23). In each composition there is a small area to which the eye is inevitably led. These are the places where shapes impinge on one another, or where they are squeezed. Imagine that they are volumes of solid matter, jostling for space or being acted on by a force. Wherever pressure appears to being applied or collision seems imminent are points of attention. Compositional nuclei, you could call them.

Remember always that all these procedures are devices; they are part of technique, and technique alone is never any good. All that matters is that you have something to say. It's always possible for someone with the right conviction to break through technical difficulties. In fact, many painters will say that technique gets in the way, and an artist is better without it. There have been many "primitive" painters, so called because they are untrained, who have supported this contention by producing beautiful and very direct paintings while doing everything wrong according to accepted technical criteria. My feeling is that these painters are exceptional, and that there are countless other amateur painters getting into difficulties with quite unnecessary and protracted technical struggles. You need just enough technique not to have to think about it too much. But I could be wrong. The thing about the arts today is that almost anything you wish to do can be all right.

We have dealt so far with the method of

moving the horizon up and down or empha-
sizing it as a compositional aid. Another
way is to turn so that land and sea share the
horizon. The variations on this theme are
endless, but the recurrent difficulty is that
such compositions tend to be heavily
weighted on the landward side and to run
away out of the picture on the seaward side.
Attention has to be held inside the picture
by some means.

Figure 24 shows, I hope, one possible solution. I have tried to clarify the main compositional ideas in the diagram in Figure 25,
and Figure 26 is the original drawing done
on the spot. It was January, very cold and
windy, sunlight and heavy cloud with rain
alternating, so that the sky and the lighting
of land and sea was changing rapidly. It
happened that I had with me only a ruled
writing pad and a felt-tipped pen. Marks
made by these pens are easily smudged by
moisture, so I made my drawing using pen,
finger, and spit!

Tonal Values

Where rain was falling from the low cloud, it
made grayish, misty columns linking land
and sky, framing bright slabs of sunlit cloud
over the further hills. At this stage, most of
the far cliff forms were in shadow, but lay-
ered in tone, so that each succeeding
promontory was sharply defined against the
next by a subtle but distinct change of tone.
Middleground and foreground appeared by
contrast to be much lighter, although in fact
the tone was still quite dark compared with
bright areas of the sky, and broken water at
the distant shorelines. Incidentally, it is easy
to be misled when assessing tonal values if
you allow your view to become too concen-
trated. A close examination of an overall
low-tone area will reveal to the human eye
(which is very good at adjusting to low-light
conditions) a great range of discern-

23. The composition in each diagram shows the area to which the eye is led, thus creating different eye levels.

ible tone. Before making too much of these changes, however, you should compare them with the brightest areas to find their true value. The probability is that those changes which seemed extreme when you looked at them alone, will be quite subtle when related to the view as a whole.

In this case the darkest tones were in the middleground and slightly to the left of center, making a strong contrast to the light area of broken water. Thus three big forms—two land and one sea—come together; and just at this junction there is a small, black rock silhouetted against the form—a very useful centering point. Also helping to stop the viewer's interest sliding off to the right is the rock outcrop jutting from the sea on the right; it works as a full stop, and the line of breakers from it links with the main area of breaking waves. Recording the sky at that particular moment in time, when two columns of rain frame the picture area, helps center attention, too. All these elements exist in the natural scene, but the choices that can be made of view position, selection of picture area, and lighting conditions can make all the difference, and this is before exploring the possibilities of emphasis or even distortion.

A comparable compositional device was used in the picture in the step-by-step series (Figures 27, 28, and 29). The only real incident here is the almost geometrically square-cut channel between the big cliff and the rock at its foot. Rock strata and beach pebble patterns were interesting, but not sufficient without this central point of tension.

25. (Above) The compositional diagram is an analysis of the pattern of the painting in Fig. 24.

24. (Left) This painting shows the land and the sea sharing the same horizon line, and the attention point is on the rocks which prevents the emphasis being put solely on the landward side.

27. (Above) **Rocky Beachscape**, Step 1. Here the composition is blocked in. The square-cut channel between the rock and cliff is the focal point on the horizon line. Thin washes were laid in to indicate the water.

26. (Left) This was the original felt-pen drawing of the scene for the painting in Fig. 24.

28. (Above) **Rocky Beachscape**, Step 2. The darks are deepened and the water is more defined.

29. (Right) **Rocky Beachscape**, Step 3. Highlights are painted on the rock strata and beach pebble patterns are added. But the central point is still the cliff and rock formation.

30. To create an interesting composition with a flat horizon, objects such as ropes and boats can be placed in the foreground.

Patterns

Another way to deal with the pervasive flat horizon is to break it with a foreground object, a large rock, or perhaps a boat (Figure 30). This method usually requires a low eye level, probably necessitating a viewpoint down on the beach. While you are walking along a beach or quay, be open to the patterns made against the sea background by objects passed (Figure 31). Unless a conscious effort is made to these possibilities of pattern, the eye only sees *either* the near objects *or* the horizon, depending on focus, and rarely correlates the two. Try changing your eye level from standing to crouching or sitting, move to right and left and see how the foreground-background pattern changes. A group of boats on a far quay, which when viewed directly may be a little dull, often takes on a new dimension when viewed through and past the rigging and superstructure of a nearer boat; or when framed by bollards, ropes, etc. Perhaps from one of the higher streets of a seaside town a little microcosm of harbor and boats—all color and activity—can be glimpsed between two buildings, and the very narrowness and isolation of the view can somehow heighten its intensity.

Perspective

Apart from compositional shape, the sea has a three-dimensional shape of its own. Its depth we cannot normally see, but its top surface is basically a horizontal plane. If a convincing illusion of recession and space is what one wants, rather than flat pattern, then it is essential to try to make the plane of the sea lie at a right angle relative to the land, and not to stand up like a wall. It is not easy: unlike a box, the sea has no parallel edges to which we can apply perspective; but like a boarded floor, it has a patterned surface (usually anyway, unless it is flat calm, which is even more difficult to portray in painting.

Wave patterns are rendered progressively smaller and more compressed the farther away they are. Careful observation and rendering of this gives a very strong sense of the plane of the sea. Shapes of white broken water which function as areas of pattern in perspective also help the illusion, again, as long as they are acutely observed. Jetties and breakwaters define an edge, and a succession of beaches getting smaller and flatter as they recede suggest a plane that otherwise featureless sea is assumed to follow.

Cloud shadows, which are more compressed nearer the horizon (as are the clouds themselves), changes of color in the sea (usually intensifying as it recedes, but not always so), the perspective of any floating object, raft, boat can all contribute to telling how the horizontal plane lies.

Boats are very useful, especially in the foreground, where other perspective clues are diminished. If the shape of the boat in itself and at the waterline is well drawn, the plane of the water is made apparent, and if this apparent surface is confirmed by a second object, farther away for instance, it becomes really positively placed in a three-dimensional plane.

31. A group of objects such as boats lined along a quay creates patterns which make an interesting composition.

bright tops
warm grey

← low light

haze, bluey

seaweed

wave cuts

grey green

strata lines

as wave recedes
water pours off these
rocks

foam area

10:30 am. January

seawall

CHAPTER FOUR

The mobile sea

When the painter looks away from the solidity of the land out to the vast stretches of water that cover most of the earth, he has to come to terms with a basic disparity between his art and the reality. The painting is static, the sea is on the move.

That statement, like most statements, is only partly true. The inferred difference in mobility between land and sea is really only a matter of time scale, as the earth is on the move too. It never stops; the land masses shift and slide and grind against each other, rearing up in collision, interior material oozing out of the cracks to form subterranean mountain ranges—but it all happens slowly in a human time scale.

Studying the Moving Sea

Although all the effects of the movement are there to see, nothing changes during the time that it takes to paint a picture. Neither is it true to say that the real bulk of the sea is very mobile. As far as we know, the vast volumes of deep water don't move very much or very quickly. If they did, the marine horizon would not look as flat as it usually does. Where the sea is really on the move is in the upper layers, especially at the surface, and at the edges where it contacts the land. Even when conditions of flat calm pervade, there is some lapping on the beach or creeping of tide.

When wind, currents, tides, and shoreline combine to produce waves—and this nearly all the time—events are occurring much faster than we can put them down on paper. It is no good sitting with pencil poised ready to capture the precise shape of a particular wave; it's all over and become something different before hardly a mark has been made. What can you do then? Sit and watch for a while. Discover which events are repeated, count the waves to see if there is a pattern to the incidence of extra large waves. Search out the wavelines and deter-

mine their direction in relation to the shore. Note what happens to the wave at its last stage of backwash from the shore, then look to see what is happening to the waveline immediately following it at the this stage. On the next sequence, check the next wave back again at the same stage. Note the observations either by writing or by drawing simple diagrams, or both. Next take a penultimate stage of the life of a wave, perhaps the actual impact with the shore. As before, check what the waves following are doing at this moment, especially noting impacts with rocks or promontories farther out. In this way, a complete picture of several sequences of events can be built up, so that a choice can be made later as to which sequence is best for any given composition.

Studying Waves

A purely visual, less analytical way of note-taking is represented by two sketches Color Plates 7 and 8. Here a point of impact between wave and rock was fixed, and observations made every time the event recurred, ignoring everything between. Gradually a composite portrait can be built up of a *series* of waves, each repeating the event in a similar way, so that the final wave represents the average appearance of a number of waves breaking at that point. It is comparable to an experiment in drawing we tried in an art school where I teach. Most of the students were in the center of the studio, while two others bicycled around the outer edge. Every student looked directly outward, and each time a cyclist passed, a small visual fact was recorded The passing cyclist was never quite the same, but as long as only truly seen and remembered facts were put down, an image was gradually created which represented the complete action of cycling, rather than a frozen moment.

32. Tintagel, Step 1. Visual and written notes in this sketch aid in remembering details observed in studying waves.

33. (Above) **Tintagel**, Step 2. Shapes and masses are sorted out and defined from the note sketch. Placement of horizon and top of the rock on a coinciding level was intentional so that attention is focused on the waves below.

Color Plate 1. (Right) **Rough Sea at Tintagel**, Step 3, oil on illustration board, 13¼″ x 18¼″. The third stage shows shadow areas worked in transparent, thin paint. Clogged-up areas of opaque paint are scraped to the surface. Light areas are heavily built up with impasto, adding to the painting's brightness and solidity.

Color Plate 2. (Left) **Rolling Waves**, watercolor on illustration board, 10½″ x 13½″. The sea can be almost any color; it reflects the sky and is most often a green-blue hue. The white of the caps has been discriminately painted so that the waves do not look frozen.

Color Plate 3. (Right) **Waves and Rocks**, oil on illustration board, 10″ x 10½″. Tones and shapes are carefully sorted out in this painting so that the sea's assault upon the solidity of the rocks is strongly suggested.

Color Plate 4. (Left) **Beach Strata, Kilve, North Somerset**, gouache on illustration board, 14½″ x 20½″. On seacoasts where there are strata at the cliff face, beautiful, rhythmic patterns follow down to the beaches.

34. (Right) This diagram shows the cycle of wave collisions: (1) shows waveline A hitting the edge of the cliff, then waveline B follows with a shallow trough between them; (2) shows waveline A advancing and deflecting against the cliff as the head-on collision water begins to backwash; (3) shows waveline A has gone farther onto the lower rocks, curling itself on the beach shelves. The backwash from the cliff begins to collide with advancing waveline B.

36. (Above) This photograph, taken at 1/1000th second, reveals a breaking wave similar to the shapes in Hokusai's woodcut (Fig. 35).

35. (Left) From **The Thirty-six Views of Fuji** by Katsushika Hokusai. This woodcut, one of thirty-six views, shows that the artist has studied carefully the movement of waves, yet it contains the artist's "super real" interpretation of the seascape.

Taking Notes and Making Sketches

Figure 32 is not so much a drawing as a combination of visual and written notes put down as it happens on a piece of writing paper. Whenever you are confronted with anything which interests you visually, and which you think could make an interesting painting, make a note of it somehow on any scrap of paper, old envelope, or whatever is available. It is essential to supplement your memory with something actually put down on paper. Even if the notes are lost, there is something about drawing a thing which impresses it in your memory in a way that no amount of observation can match.

After making these first notes of principal shapes, I spent about half an hour watching the waves pounding against the near vertical cliff. There is no possibility of drawing the surf as it happens, of course, so the only way is to look for the repeated patterns of shape. It was quite easy in this case to analyze the sequence of events. Well-defined waves seemed to be coming in groups of six or seven. The exact number doesn't matter to us, and the distance between the wavelines was roughly equivalent to the height of the cliff. (Judging dimensions relatively to each other is better than attempting to estimate actual lengths in feet.) One or two waves in each group were detectable quite far out, and as they approached would begin to break at the crest, the wind catching and blowing the spray shoreward. As the first of these waves hit the cliff, it would be hurled straight up by the impact with the jutting corner, then, having been split, it would be deflected along the side of the cliff facing me in a sort of rolling, progressive break like that around the bows of a moving ship. Immediately following this would be the backwash forming a concavity of white water, leaving hundreds of miniature mountain torrents streaming from the small rocks at the foot of the cliff.

As the following wave met the backwash, there would be a minor collision which only served to pile the oncoming wave higher still, so that when it hit the cliff the explosion of brilliant white water would tower up nearly to the top of the cliff. It was astonishing how slowly and with what impression of great weight this tower was erected, slowed, paused, and then fell back into the sea, almost like a slow-motion film. The area of the sea surface which was white maintained a remarkably regular shape, and could therefore be quite precisely delineated. Figure 34 is a series of diagrams which shows stages in the cycle of wave collisions as described above, Diagram 1 shows a wave of waveline A impacting the sharp edge of the cliff, the next waveline B following up with a fairly flat shallow trough between. Diagram 2 shows the waveline A continuing to advance, breaking across the cliff in a deflection, while the head-on collision water is already falling back and beginning to backwash. In the third wave A has progressed further and is now swelling up over lower rocks and curling over on itself as the beach shelves, while the backwash from the cliff is now strong and in collision with the advancing waveline B. The cycle then begins again with wave B hitting the cliff in its turn.

Wave Patterns

It would be nice if we could somehow show all these stages in one painting, and indeed there is no reason why not. Overlaying the progressive patterns to get a sense of movement can be experimented with, but if that seems unacceptably unrealistic, a moment in time can be picked, and the motion to that position suggested by the rhythm of the line and pattern of shape on shape.

That may sound complicated but it isn't really; it's just a matter of feeling the way

that the waves are moving and letting your brush move with the same rhythm.

Anyway, if we treat as stage one all the drawings done on the spot, including the stage analysis sketches of the waves, then the compositional construction (Figure 33) is stage two. Here the disposition of the main masses has been sorted out, so as to establish the positions of tension points as centers of attention. As I said earlier, the coincidence of horizon and the top of the rock was intentional, so as to concentrate attention below the horizon on the waves.

After that, the problem was to sort out tones and shapes in such a way as to suggest the solidity of the rock and the constant movement of the sea's assault. The treatment in the later stages is a matter for individual choice, but it is likely to be more manageable if the thickest paint is saved until the last. Shadow areas work best in transparent, comparatively thin paint, and if such areas get out of control and become clogged with a build-up of thick opaque paint, it may be necessary to scrape down to the surface and try again. Light areas, on the other hand, may benefit from heavily built-up layers of paint (called impasto), as the rough edges catch the light, adding to the brightness of the area and increasing the effect of solidity (Color Plate 1).

Making a "Statement"

I took some photographs as well, but they were not much referred to. They were taken as a safeguard—a source of extra factual information in case of need. Beware of using one single photograph of breaking waves

37. Snowstorm, J.M.W. Turner. Atmosphere is the dominant theme here. Light juxtaposes with the darkest dark in the center of vision, which is a familiar Turner theme. (The Tate Gallery, London)

38. Firsthand observation of breaking waves and moving water is the best method for depicting them as shown in this felt-pen sketch.

as reference, for it records a split-second event and gives no clue about the moments before or after. without some knowledge of the mobile pattern, it is very difficult to select and simplify, and consequently difficult to make a personal statement. To speak about "statements" in painting seems strange and inappropriate to many people. I think it means—in objective painting at least—that by selecting some particular aspect of light or shape or form, you say to an observer not only that "I was at this place," but also that "I discovered *this* about this place which pleased / terrified / amused me." In other words, "This is how I felt about this thing that I saw, do you recognize the feeling?" I am quite sure this is not a complete explanation of the esthetic experience, but at one level I think some such striking of a chord which means experience shared, or vicarious experience which a person believes in because other parts ring true, is the basis of most people's response to a painting.

I suppose that one of the most popular types of sea painting with the buying public is a picture showing a wave rolling in toward the viewer, thinning near its crest so that sunlight glints through the pale green, and further along the wave it curls and breaks in bundles of white foam. Now it is true that this is how waves *do* sometimes appear, but if you know the paintings I refer to, perhaps you will understand what I mean when I say that there is something very superficial about them. It is a show of dexterity, like saying, "Look, I can paint this wave to look transparent," and is in the same category as "Look, I can paint this eye so that it looks watery and real." In both cases, the superficial trick is very easy, the more *difficult* thing that all good painters go for is making a complete painting, only using such things as glinting sunlight through a wave and highlights in the eye if they are really appropriate to the painting, and not just an eye-catching trick.

The point of this is not to condemn these painters—they could be right, and everyone decides for himself how he paints—but to suggest they are not good models for the amateur artist. Apart from the question of whether or not commercially popular sea paintings are worthwhile, I am quite sure that to copy them would be disastrous. The sea itself must be the source, and if other painters' work is copied it should only be as an exercise to discover how *they* solved the problem. In this case, keep to the masters. Go to a national collection of paintings for guidance and influence, not to the picture department of the local store.

A Few Pitfalls to Avoid

Having said before that there are no rules, I will now summarize a few things—especially related to the sea on the move—which I think are rather dangerous and probably better avoided at least at first. Avoid painting violently breaking waves entirely from a photograph. The action will be frozen and the painting will have no feel of the dynamics of the incident.

Do not pile thick white paint indiscriminately on a seascape in order to make the sea look rough. Observation of the form of waves in a rough sea, and the characteristic shape of foam areas, is much more likely to be effective.

Try not to acquire pet methods for depicting moving water which are based on preconceptions. Try instead to come to the sea with an open mind, ready to discover something entirely new every time.

Do not depend on other artists' observations, whoever the artists may be. Especially do not copy the sort of paintings which show wave "white horses" changing into real white horses and galloping out of the sea!

Some Great Sea Paintings

I would like in this context to talk about two of what I consider to be great sea paintings. The Hokusai woodcut (Figure 35) is one of a series of thirty-six views of Fujiyama produced during the period 1823—29, before photography, I would point out. Figure 36 is my photograph of a breaking wave, exposed at 1/1000th second and revealing remarkably similar shapes of flying foam.

I suspect that there is no valid inference to be drawn, but I like to think that it shows how right a great artist can be, using a combination of observation and creativity. Hokusai has looked at the sea, and knows all about how water moves, you can tell that; but he has not produced a "realistic" picture. It is more "super real"—his idea of the vitality and force of the sea. The men and their wave-shaped boats are not immediately noticeable; they are overpowered by the great wave in form, and perhaps in a moment to be overwhelmed in fact. But besides this, the whole thing is very beautiful to look at, the composition artfully contrived so that distant Fuji still somehow commands the whole scene. The mountain stands quite aloof from the marine drama, strangely similar to the wave in shape, but not to be mistaken for a moment for anything but a static land shape.

A very different attitude is exemplified by the Turner painting (Figure 37). Here atmosphere, not form, is the primary interest. Turner, at this stage, was pursuing the substance and texture of air itself, stressing its presence all around us, and the necessity to look through it at the world. Water vapor, smoke, spray, steam, and in this case snow interested him, and the interplay of light diffused through the atmosphere or reflected in water. There are others of his paintings which exemplify this more clearly than this one, and which I would have preferred to show, but they are mostly so dependent on infinitely subtle misty gradations of color that they do not reproduce well in black and white. Tonal contrast in this picture is stronger than most of this period, so that even in black and white the color can be sensed, the wetness of the water felt. Having the most brilliant light for juxtaposition with the darkest dark in the center of vision is a familiar Turner idea, and you may have noticed other compositional aids in the form of wavelines and clouds which point to the center of interest. I *think* it is a paddle steamer struggling along in the heavy seas, its mast silhouetted against the light, but I'm not entirely sure, and I don't think it matters too much.

CHAPTER FIVE
The shore

Although the sea itself is rarely still, and for this reason a little difficult to observe and draw, the effects of its movements are clear to see in the shaping of beaches and cliffs. A marvelously complete and explicit record of the continuous activity of the sea is written there, in the shore, for all who understand the language. I know very little of this language, and I would not expect everyone who aspired to paint sea and shore first to study geology. Much is obvious though, even to an untutored eye.

Studying Shoreline Rocks

Some of the most remarkable sea-eroded rocks I have seen are on the Atlantic coasts of the Isles of Scilly, although there are, no doubt, many others like them on unprotected oceanic coasts throughout the world. Thousands or even millions of years of pounding seas have worn these coasts into a fantastic array of strange shapes. It is hard rock, granite in the main, and it hasn't fallen easily. It has withstood the barrage long enough to have been shaped infinitesimally slowly into magnificently varied monumental forms. When I first saw these rocks it was summer, but they were under the sort of attack which is normal during the winter—enormous, crashing waves, gale force winds, a constant thunderous noise. It was impossible to draw there, but very exciting to watch. A couple of days afterwards the weather reverted to summer calm, the sea was blue and clear. It was difficult to believe that the benign and balmy water could ever have been any different. Except for the rocks; there they were, battered and twisted, and you knew that you hadn't imagined all that ferocity. However mild the sea looked now, the rocks proclaimed loud and clear that this coast was a wild one, an Atlantic coast, not to be trifled with.

Some of the rocks shaped by the sea take forms which are rounded and smooth in line, like great pieces of sculpture (which is what they are, I suppose, only without human intervention). These shapes are not random, they are the result of continuously repeated scourings, which, at a rate so slow as to be difficult for us even to contemplate, have transformed hard, angular rock into sea forms, with all the sweeps and curves, crusts and troughs of waves themselves. I find them very beautiful and satisfying to look at. I also think that when you draw them you must give them the same acute attention, the same critical eye for proportion and balance, as when you are drawing the human figure.

You may find other rocks which resemble fantastic architecture. Figure 39 shows a small headland that looks just like a mosque, with turrets and central dome. These types of rock, I assume from the number of crisscrossing fissures, are more inclined to become undermined, to fracture and collapse, so that they don't stand sufficiently long to become hollowed and rounded, only long enough for the sharpness of corners and edges to be softened. Again they should be lovingly observed, and not treated as a heap of haphazardly shaped lumps. Of course, no one is going to be able to say "That doesn't look like that rock," as they can say of a drawing of a horse or a figure that it looks wrong, but if for this reason you allow your vision to become sloppy and superficial, it will show in the drawing. It will have less authority, less credibility.

Using Your Imagination

Once you have extracted the vital shapes and volume of a particular piece of shoreline, there is nothing to stop you treating it in a rather imaginative way, and creating something from these ingredients which is

39. Rock Structure, Isles of Scilly. The rock structure resembles architecture whose small, mosquelike headland and fissures with softened edges require perceptive study to draw.

a long way from straightforward realism.

I did the drawing (Figure 41) sitting in front of those rocks, and I believe it is a fairly accurate statement of the rhythms and forms that were there. Looking at it later, two years later in fact, I thought it had a slightly eerie, moonlit look to it. A drop of coffee or something, which may or may not be visible in the reproduction, had fallen on the drawing, just above the horizon, and looked like a heavenly orb, which may have added to the impression. I thought it might be interesting to develop the drawing into a more imaginative design by using the forms I had discovered from the actuality.

The second stage was a color rough (Color Plate 5), in which I tried to decide how best to use solid tones to express what was previously linear. I am not too keen personally on popping the sun or the moon haphazardly into pictures as a compositional prop. It has been done so much that it has become something of a cliché, but there are occasions when it seems appropriate, and this seemed to be one of those occasions. Sun or moon always give an added dimension, an extra air of mystery, perhaps because they point to the existence of unknown worlds outside our own, but it is an easy trick and it will lose its power if used too often.

I felt that the third stage should not be a painting as such, but something which would allow several combinations of color and tone to be tried and compared for maximum effect, which meant using one of the many print methods.

---

40. Sand Dunes. A careful composition was made in this wash drawing. The water, hill, and sky are in the background; the sand and beach flora in the foreground with their rich detail draw the eye to the foreground.

Monoprinting

Probably the simplest method to apply paint, other than by brushing it on, is to spread the paint on glass or some other flat surface and press it to the painting surface, either through a cut mask or without. Color so applied has a distinct quality of its own which, although it can vary greatly (depending on how the paint is applied to the glass, the pressure when transferring, the type and thickness of paint, etc.), never looks the same as paint directly brushed on. It is a print method and is usually called monoprinting. I started the third stage (Color Plate 6) of this little picture of the rocks by applying broad areas of color in this way.

It is usually only possible to obtain two or three prints at the most from any one application of paint to the glass, and each print made is much paler than the previous one. To ensure exact registration of successive printings on any one version, it is a good ideas to tape the paper in position by one edge.

While paint is applied to the glass, the paper can be flapped back out of the way, but because it is permanently attached, it will always be pressed onto the glass in exactly the same position. Up to four pictures could progress at the same time in this way, one folding each from top and bottom, and one from each side. Of course, registration can be achieved by marking the position of the corners of the sheets of paper, which marks can then be used to reposition it and any number of other sheets of the same size.

Most types of paint will transfer in this way, but printing inks—which are oil-bound and rather tacky—are usually best, especially if applied by roller and printed with some pressure. Acrylics are usable, but the quick drying makes printing a matter of speed and timing.

In general, a lot more paint is used when monoprinting than in painting direct, so be

prepared for an expensive time, with bulk quantities.

Many Facets of Seascapes

The watercolor painting (Color Plate 11) represents an entirely different kind of shoreline. Actually the sketch in Figure 40 shows more clearly how the area looks in general. It is a sandy bay with a very shallow sloping beach, straddled by areas of low dark-colored rocks. They are the same rocks in each, viewed from much closer in the color picture. This beach is backed by dunes, which are constantly being blown further inland by the prevailing wind, and which support tufty growths of a dry reed-like grass. It is one of those beaches where the tide always seems to be out, I suppose because it goes out so far that only when it is fully flooding does it seem within reach at all.

It is a wide open and often windswept place, the sea rolls in and dissipates its sometimes considerable energies on the flat sand. There is no thunderous battle between wave and cliff; it is the wind that has most to do with the changing shoreline here. In fact, it was this watercolor that I referred to in the materials chapter, talking about the difficulties of painting in a high wind.

The wind here was unbelievable—not hurricane force perhaps, but enough to make me feel (as it sometimes seems in particularly nasty conditions) that the elements are somehow directed against me personally and malevolently. The worst part was the bombardment of needle like particles of sand, which drove into every crevice, into the paint, into water and brushes—but I stuck it out, I say smugly, and perhaps the situation made me work more urgently. Certainly it did not take long; the washes dried almost as soon as they were laid, and al-

41. (Above) **Rock, Isles of Scilly**, Step 1. This drawing was done at the exact location. Sometime later, an accidental drop of coffee fell on the drawing and helped to create an eerie mood.

Color Plate 5. (Right) **Rock, Isles of Scilly**, Step 2, color rough, 4¾″ x 7½″. The second stage of this scene is a color rough in which the solid tones are used to express more than the linear quality and the moon gives dimension to the composition.

Color Plate 7. (Above) **Wave Study I**, watercolor on illustration board, 8¼″ x 12¾″. In this sketch, a composite portrait was made, built up of a series of waves.

Color Plate 6. (Left) **Rocks, Isles of Scilly**, Step 3, monoprint, 10½″ x 15″. The third stage was done by painting watercolor on glass. The glass was pressed onto the printing surface, transferring the paint.

though I must say it doesn't look very windy, the dune grass clumps took on wind-blown shapes which I think are rather nice. Designers' gouache, watercolors, on heavy, rough-surface, handmade paper (unstretched) were used for this watercolor, incidentally.

Such conditions are not all that unusual by the sea, and it is quite impossible to work unless everything is firmly anchored in place and the artist himself is well protected. Using an easel is out of the question, and lots of tape or clips are necessary to hold paper to board. One hand can then hold the board as steady as possible, water jar wedged in sand or cleft of rock, and paintbox heavy enough to stand on its own, preferably with a firm prop for the open lid. The palette is a problem, but in bad conditions I usually resort to a piece of cardboard extended outward to right or left of the board on which I am working. This is then firmly held by the "board holding" hand.

You are tempted to wonder whether all this trouble is worth taking. I think that it is. If you work only in clement weather, the real character of the sea will be misrepresented, and there will be many less opportunities to work and to make new discoveries. In fact, I feel that bright sunlight sometimes *obscures* the vital character of a place. There have been times when I have sat down to paint a rocky shoreline which, under a cloudy sky, was all strong sculptured forms, telling of great earth pressures and subsequent bombardment by tons of water, only to find when the sun came out and shone prettily on it all, that it suddenly

Color Plate 8. **Wave Study II**, watercolor on illustration board, 8¼" x 12¾". Notes were made of the impact of waves on rocks and promontories farther out, A complete picture of several sequences was built up, and the choice of the best sequence led to this composition.

looked benign and characterless. Surface forms become more obviously apparent of course, but the underlying general structure is obscured. This does not always apply; quite as often strong light *reveals* underlying big forms, but my point is that for the best picture, a blue sky and bright sunlight are not obligatory. There is a sort of cliché linking the seaside with summer sun which, I must admit, tempts me to concentrate on the severer aspects of the sea.

Occasionally, I have included in this book subjects which are not strictly seascapes, but I believe this to be justified by such subjects being directly connected with, shaped by, or strongly reminiscent of the sea.

While walking on a cliff top looking for interesting rock forms this summer, I saw, perched on the hillside inland of the cliff, a group of what seemed to be most interesting sea-formed rocks: or was it a sculpture or driftwood? When I moved closer, I saw that it was the skull of some species of whale, parts of which had come adrift and lay where they had fallen. Someone had mounted it on a rock and propped the end of the long jaw on a small pillar of brick, so that it pointed out to sea.

It had a striking monumental quality and an incredible similarity in the character of its form to the gale-eroded rocks of the Scilly Isles (Figure 42).

It would probably be fanciful to endow this similarity with great significance, but I think one should be alive to such things—fanciful or not—and always receptive to visual stimuli from any source, even though the primary objective may be only to paint the sea itself.

This particular subject may also serve to illustrate what I have said about mere accurate copying not really being enough. My first quick painting done on the spot seemed to have no bulk and to have missed completely the monumental look, so I tried

to analyze the main movements in a simpler way in a pen and wash drawing (Figure 43). This still missed the point, and a return was made to the spot to try to sort out the underlying strength of the forms. I found I had to increase contrasts, simplify surface detail, and unify and darken the background; in fact, completely repaint with more assertion and less slavish copying of the surface reality. The final painting (Color Plate 14) while still falling far short of the presence of the actual object, is nearer to it.

Painting Outdoors versus Comfort

Figure 44 and Color Plate 12 are two drawings of the same subject drawn from exactly the same viewpoint, but made on successive days. On the first day the sea was calm and the sky uniformly overcast, although the light was quite bright. The pattern of growth and fissures on the cliff face made a sort of frieze separating a flat sea and a flat sky. Next day the weather had worsened; skies were dark and lowering, and the wind was almost gale force. To paint outside in such conditions was impossible, but fortunately I was able to position my car (dangerously near the edge) so that the cliff could be seen through the windshield and the painting was done from the front passenger seat. When you paint outdoors, it is always debatable whether personal comfort or exactly the right viewpoint, however uncomfortable, should take precedence. My feeling is that, in general, I should be well enough equipped to be able to make myself comfortable in the *right* position, but that if this is really impossible it is silly to stick it out with freezing hands, running eyes, and the increasingly urgent necessity of taking shelter—and expect to produce anything good. Wind, spray, and light rain can be braved, but cold is something else. Rather than get really cold, better make a few notes to be amplified in the studio from memory, or else retire to a more sheltered spot—even a car—and draw whatever can be seen from there.

Searching for the Right View

There is a road not far from where I live in the southwest of England which, at a certain high point, presents a sudden wide view of the coast which always comes rather as a surprise. I have driven along the road many times, and yet I am always caught a little unprepared; and although I want to stop and look for a few moments, there always seems to be a car following close behind, and by the time I am able to slow down and stop, the high vantage point has passed and I tend to think that it will probably be even nicer as the road nears the coast. It isn't; there is just not another comparable view of this unusual coastline.

The point of this little story is that we should grasp the opportunities that present themselves. So often we go on and on looking for a viewpoint that is just a little better, only to end up with no drawing at all. If you pass a view that seems in retrospect to be promising, go back and have another look.

I still haven't made a painting of my surprise vista, but I did at least manage to stop at the top of the hill and make a small pen sketch (Figure 45). What I tried to analyze was the special quality that this vista had that hit me each time. On reflection, it seemed that it was partly a matter of changes of level and plane. The curving, downhill stretch of road was important to it, and so was the curvy, wooded hill in the middleground. Then the flat plain, with its

42. Rocks, Isles of Scilly. The monumental quality of the rocks was captured in pen and ink in this sketch.

43. Whale's Head. This second attempt in pen and ink still did not quite capture the main movement and bulk of the whale's head propped up on a pile of bricks. Color Plate 14 is the third attempt in painting the same scene again, and that version comes closer to the feeling of the scene.

44. Bigbury Cliff, Calm Day. The same scene as in Color Plate 12 but done on a calm, uniformly overcast day, shows the cliff—friezelike—separating sea from sky.

45. (Left) **Chesil Bank, Dorest.** This pen and ink sketch shows the changes of plane in the curving road and the flat horizon which created an interesting composition with the sea.

46. (Right) **Slipway, Croyde, North Devon.** The sea framed by the two jetties gives a definite feeling of distance and depth.

47. (Above) **Chalk Cliffs, Saltdean.** This pen and ink wash drawing is another fine example of outdoor drawing.

48. (Right) When rock strata are not concealed by sand, they make interesting textures for sketches as in this pencil drawing.

straight beach and shingle bank running dead parallel seemed to tilt up toward me, the horizon (on this day at least) being only a misty blur. Each time I see it, it looks different, and I expect a few more drawings will be made at different times of the day and seasons of the year, before I really get it sorted out.

Rock strata on the beach are usually concealed by shingle or sand—but not always. There are seacoasts where the strata visible at the cliff face can be followed down into the surface of the beach itself. Such a foreshore is the subject of the drawing in Color Plate 4. Down from the cliff top, there is a continuous succession of beautiful patterns over several miles of beach. With such explicit patterns as these, it is difficult to draw generalized forms.

In this case, the main shapes were first put down in watered-down sepia ink and brush, the detailed pattern being built up with darker glazes of sepia ink and opaque whites and grays. At the time the light was very flat, so that the elements of the pattern owed little or nothing to cast shadows. The area of light and shade related instead to the interplay of strata lines, and the standing water contained within them. As the striations are traced further into the picture onto the far beaches, they are seen to define the undulating form of the foreshore, and their decreasing scale gives a sense of distance.

Long views of the coast and beaches, although fascinating, are not the only rewarding aspects of shoreline. There is a world of closer, more intimate beachscapes, made up of rock pools, driftwood, flotsam and jetsam of all kinds.

Other Objects in Compositions

There are beautiful compositions to be found even in such unlikely things as the floating scum and debris that collects in harbors sometimes, or in the tangles of rope and rusty equipment. To change gear visually, and focus on the microcosm of pebbles and shells, can open up a whole new set of possibilities. Sometimes it is possible to forget your size and imagine that the miniature seascape of the rock pool is the norm, so closely does it resemble full-size topography. There is something very peaceful and satisfying about gently wandering along the tideline, searching for interesting objects, picking up rock after interesting rock, pieces of cork float, colored glass, and pottery abraded into pebble shapes, wood shapes looking as though they have been carefully sculpted and smoothed—until the load becomes ridiculously heavy and all but the very nicest pieces are regretfully dropped.

When your treasures are laid out at home, they re-create the beach; they are so obviously of the sea, so different from inland objects. Why not set them up as a still life? And if your painting of these sea-shaped things begins to resemble a fanciful marinescape, that's fine. This is one of the delights of painting; images can be mixed in time and place; it really isn't obligatory to place everything in a picture strictly in the context in which it was seen in one moment. You should feel free to arrange elements as you feel they are important, or just as you would like them to be. There are *no* rules that must be obeyed in painting.

Color Plate 9. **Wet Beach**, oil on illustration board, 10″ x 16″. In this sketch, the breaking waves form an eye-holding pattern in the middleground. The flowing water on the sand near the two figures help to create an interesting placement of the horizon line.

Color Plate 11. (Above) **Study of Shoreline**, watercolor on textured board, 16″ x 21″. This painting of the beach backed by dunes and windswept sand was done in high winds, which created a changing shoreline. The sea's rolling and ebbing also helped change the shoreline.

Color Plate 10. (Left) **Kilve Cliffs, North Somerset**, oil on illustration board, 14¾″ x 16″. This painting proves that orderly palette layout is important for mixing of hues. The greens, browns, and blues are clear, touched with warm highlights of yellow and burnt sienna.

CHAPTER SIX

Flora and fauna

Color Plate 12. **Bigbury Cliff, Stormy Day**, watercolor on textured board, 13¼″ x 18½″. The same scene as Fig. 44 was painted the following day when the weather had worsened. Skies were darker and the wind was of gale force, creating a definite color change.

While you are searching the foreshore for interesting objects, inevitably you will find life forms themselves. There are very few beaches without some shells, and the diversity of size, shape, and color is very great, and they are all beautiful.

Shells

In Figure 49, the little striped shells are types of periwinkle, some of which are minute and brightly colored, mostly yellow, orange, and red. The spiral object at top left is a fossil of an ammonite. They are quite common in certain coastal rocks of Dorset, and lived in the seas 170 million years ago!

Crustaceans

Crabs are all too often represented as vaguely circular pink bodies bristling with rubbery legs, two of which end in nasty little pincers. The same applies to lobsters, crayfish, and many other common sea creatures. It seems we only look at these animals in the context of their threat to us; they pinch us, therefore they are walking pincers.

In fact, they are really rather beautiful too. Those fearsome pincers, although they *can* do damage, are also used as delicate eating utensils (Figure 51). The jointing of the main claws of crabs and lobsters is a marvelous solution to the problem of movement when the skeleton is on the outside. A close and careful look at these creatures (who, incidentally, have been around a lot longer than man) shows them to be very delicately and neatly organized, well adapted to life in the sea, and very rewarding to draw (Figure 52).

Seaweed

Rock pools are probably the most easily available source of varied sea life material.

The water is usually clear and not too deep, sea anemones open up and variegated seaweeds look healthy and colorful—unlike the rather dank heaps that are left high and dry by the retreating tide.

Subaquatic Views

There is, of course, a whole vast other world below the sea's surface, the measure of which we are only just beginning to realize. Anyone who has explored this underwater world with the aid of scuba equipment, as I have, knows the absolute "otherness" of this element, once the surface has become the ceiling, shutting out the world of air, wind, sound, smell, and above all gravity. Subaquatic views have as much variety of topography and flora as land ones, as long as the sun can penetrate, but as the sea floor descends to depths where sunlight cannot reach, it appears more and more barren. We know that the water itself teems with life, but since it is mostly microscopic, and plant life is entirely absent, it doesn't look very hospitable.

In relatively shallow water, where the light is bright, the diver gradually becomes less fearful of the strange element, and can eventually feel quite at home moving weightless in this fascinating world. Perhaps such scenes, although beautiful, are not yet familiar to enough people for paintings of the underwater to have any universal meaning; and painting on the spot presents problems!

I think though that there is something to be said for seeing the other nine-tenths of the iceberg—the broad calm base of rocks which, at their surface-breaking tips, are all flurry and foaming water; the quiet valleys floored with bright sand and ringed with gently waving forests, where you can lie still and not know that at the surface the breakers are piling up and rushing at the shore.

49. Shells—because of their shape, size, and color—are plentiful on beaches and are beautiful subjects to paint.

50. Pencil sketches of variously shaped shells such as this one make good exercises for drawing in light and dark.

51. Claws of crabs and lobsters are exciting subjects too.

52. When your initial apprehension disappears, the study of the structure of lobsters can be very rewarding to draw as in this pen and ink sketch.

Fish

Most of us, most of the time, relate the sea with the shore. We observe the sea from the land, and are fascinated by the line where the two great elements of land and sea contact each other. For this reason, I think, it is the flora and fauna between the tidelines which strongly evoke the atmosphere of the sea. Fish which can never emerge from the sea and live, seem, as they lie lifeless on the fishmonger's slab, to have a different meaning.

They are lovely things mostly, but so much more attractive in the sea and alive; on land they somehow just become so much food. This is a purely personal and perhaps isolated view. I am sure that many people will feel quite differently, but a still life of fish just doesn't have the same strong evocation of my times by the sea, as for example, a crab's claw, a shell, or a piece of driftwood has.

One thing to remember if you *do* decide to paint a fishy still life; pay particular attention to the actual color, especially of the bright scales. Because fish are rather shiny, the temptation is to cover them with highlights. Resist it; observe the bright areas dispassionately. Although subjectively the scales all look shimmery, it is probable that most of the area is really quite a positive tone and color, the truly white highlights being limited to a small area.

Painting from Our Own Sea Experiences

We must realize that our feelings about the sea and its life depend very greatly on our own experience in relation to the sea. An Eskimo carves seals from the bones of the animals themselves, but although I know that seals live in and by the sea, and I also know or can find out what they look like, they do not form part of my sea experience and so have no strong evocations.

53. Driftwood, rocks, and seaweed form beautiful compositions.

54. Seaside flora is part of everyone's experience and they can certainly be easily studied and painted as in this watercolor sketch.

CHAPTER SEVEN

Man and the sea

If you spend much time by the sea and shore it becomes impossible to ignore the thousands of objects made by man to enable him to conquer or come to terms with the sea—things like boats and anchors, mooring lines and buoys, nets, floats, lobster pots, fishing tackle of all kinds.

They all evoke the sea and are part of the pattern of shoreline life, which so differs from inland. Because they are functional and from long experience have been refined so that they work more and more efficiently, these objects can be said to be sea-formed. Certainly they rarely strike a discordant note with the rocks and flora and fauna of the seaside, and sometimes the similarity to these natural forms is remarkable. For this reason they repay careful and close study, not so much of their details, although these can sometimes be fascinating, but of their basic forms.

Boats

Boats especially, which must float and be stable and slip through the water with as little resistance as possible, are very subtle and rewarding in shape.

They are only difficult to draw if you come to them with preconceptions about their shape. Draw what you truly see, and don't try to fit in what you see to your idea of what a boat *should* look like. If, for instance, a boat is viewed from a high, three-quarter front viewpoint, the curves of each gunwale will be very different; so do not draw them the same because you know that in plan the boat must be symmetrical. Similarly there may be rather unbelievably little of the far side of the bows visible in view of the width of the boat. Believe it. If you see it, believe it.

Try not only to see the intrinsic form of each boat, but the composite form and pattern of a cluster of them. To be conscious of the shapes *between* groups of objects is a

help to seeing the pattern of shape. After all these "shapes left" are just as important a part of your two-dimensional painting as the parts which represent the objects.

Seaside Structures

There are also the permanent structures that human beings erect when they settle by the sea. Such things as piers, landing platforms, quays, sea walls, boathouses, breakwaters, and harbors, and in the larger towns the seaside promenade (boardwalk), colored lights, fish shops, amusement parks, and bandstands. I personally prefer the objects which have been used traditionally to wrest a livelihood from the sea, rather than the shoreline exploitation of man's amusement needs. But I realize that this is a selfish attitude—after all, if *I* like to visit a beautiful place, why shouldn't everyone else, even if its beauty may be changed or even destroyed thereby? In a curious way even in the most outrageously holiday-oriented seaside towns, it is possible for an artist to find attraction and interest; and even if horror and repugnance is all you can feel, it is still valid to state this in your painting.

There should always be a point of view; you will feel awe, love, wonder, perhaps only curiosity, and perhaps, as I said, revulsion or bewilderment. Whatever it is, allow it to come through in your painting, don't let too much slavish description mask your feeling about the place. Only in the instance of complete non-reaction and boredom is it fairly certain to be unprofitable to paint.

Seaside Patterns and Colors

Ropes, cables, nets, and all the other paraphernalia of boating and fishing are almost always rich sources of pattern. In many parts of the world, boats have traditionally been painted in bright colors, and they al-

55. Manmade structures such as this pier, with pattern created from the pilings, are other fascinating seaside subjects to paint.

ways seem to be just the right colors for the place and the climate—fishermen must have an innate color sense. Even in the more serious-minded, northern fishery ports, where the basically brown or black boats are only enlivened by white painted numerals or the occasional straker line, their gear by contrast has taken on a much gayer appearance in recent years. Self-colored plastics have replaced glass and cork for floats; and nylon or Dacron are becoming universal replacements for hemp rope. Losses in fishing gear are high, and in order to minimize these losses it is useful to be able to see floats and buoys clearly and at a distance. Oranges, yellows, and reds provide the best visibility against the greens, blues, grays, and browns of the sea. Nylon ropes are usually orange too, and all these brilliant—often fluorescent—spots of color against the traditional black or brown of nets and lobster pots make most beautifully rich mosaics of color.

I am looking now at the stern section of a fishing boat in a Cornish harbor, which is really a work of art in itself. The hull of the boat is basically blue, but has been splashed with bright green paint, while scrapes and scratches have revealed darker purple underpaint. The board over the side is greenish, with the underpainted orange showing through; the gunwales are light blue, the mast is orange, the nets are black, orange, and blue with bright orange and pink floats.

There is a drawing of it (Figure 56) but you will have to take my word for the color, I'm afraid.

57. (Above) This diagram of a stream shows that although the stream is wide in actuality, it is but a thin strip (at A) compared to the foreground mass in the picture.

56. (Left) Nets, cables and ropes on trawlers are exciting to capture in pen and ink lines.

Color Plate 13. (Right) **Boats at Low Tide, Ilfracombe Harbour**, pen and ink on illustration board, 9¾" x 16⅛". The intrinsic form of each boat as well as the pattern of the group of them are shown in this pen and ink drawing. The shapes between the boats are just as important as the boats themselves.

Color Plate 15. (Above) **Headland, North Devon**, watercolor on illustration board, 14″ x 18½″. The placement of the horizon line and promontory with the muted color of the sea at the right in the background is an exciting juxtaposition of sea and shore. The warm colors of the middleground balance the dark green of the headland.

Color Plate 14. (Left) **Whale's Head**, oil on illustration board, 14½″ x 19¼″. This painting is the third attempt at capturing the essence of the whale's head propped up on a pile of bricks. Somewhat abstracted, it succeeds more than the drawing (Fig. 43) because of the simplicity of the greens supported by the red.

Selective Vision

In any case, these little cameos of color and shape abound in fishing harbors, it is only necessary to be receptive to them. Vision is very selective; it has to be—it is a tool and a defense in life. If you are walking in a street or rocky shore, the brain through your eye is making myriads of calculations of scale and distance, compensating for perspective, sorting information into useful and non-useful categories, always from the point of view of the safe and efficient progress and balance of the individual.

As artists we have to learn to look in a different way, objectively, seeing *apparent* shapes and sizes, without compensating. The simplest way I can explain the nature of this different vision is to ask you to imagine yourself approaching a small stream which you have to cross or jump. The mind, from the information given by the eye, will assess the width of the river and a judgment can be made about the possibilities of leaping it. Now to arrive at this judgment, calculations have been made, the distance to the stream edge has been assessed (not in precise terms but relatively), so that the allowance for perspective can be judged, the plane of the ground which affects eye level and therefore relationship of apparent width of the stream to its real width has been noted, and probably also parallax effects (the apparent change in perspective between one viewpoint and another; head movement will produce it). It has all been automatic and almost instantaneous, but it is vital and very accurate. It is these sorts of judgments which make the difference between life and death in a busy street.

Color Plate 16. **Location Sketch** by Alan Jessett, watercolor, wax, and ink on illustration board, 20″ x 27″. This is a more literal interpretation of the same scene in Fig. 60. The wax adds texture, giving the jetty a three-dimensional effect.

Now let us stop and look at this stream again. Postpone the problem of crossing it, and just look at it. Measure its apparent width, i.e., its *depth* in a composition (Figure 57). Although one can know that it actually is quite wide, it is only a narrow little stripe relative to the foreground mass.

There is sea and cliff beyond. The shape of the sea might make a particular pattern with the curve of the stream, perhaps the edge of the cliff coincides with the widest part of the stream shape. Foreground rocks dwarf the far cliffs. Perhaps those cliffs and the dark shape of sea coupled with sweeping beach strata make even a stronger compositional element than the stream itself. The stream is then relegated to a secondary role in the overall beachscape.

While you were thinking of crossing it, it was *the* most important thing in your vision, all attention was riveted on it and relevant surroundings, everything else was ignored. If you are asked to draw or describe the shape of the skyline cliffs after this first observation, you would find it impossible, just as impossible as recalling the skyline shapes of buildings on a regularly crossed busy street. Yet the information entered your eye; it was sifted, considered irrelevant, and therefore ignored.

For the objective painter it is the abstract, nonprocessed information which is essential—all the relationships and patterns of shape on shape, color against color, light and tone, texture, rhythm—all the things which are nonessential when making judgments related to action.

Interpretive Painting

Realistic illusions of recession and depth can be created by use of perspective, tonal and color changes, etc., but abstract shape comes first. Of course, once you have developed the capability of seeing the shapes

and forms as they are, there is no reason why they should not then be stressed or changed or distorted, if it helps to make the statement clearer and more forceful.

My drawing of boats in Ilfracombe harbor (Color Plate 13 and Figures 58 and 59) although fairly factual, have nevertheless stressed certain aspects of the reality so as to give greater importance to them than was perhaps the case in reality. In both it was the two-dimensional design that fascinated me—the pattern of solid shapes crisscrossed by masts, booms, rigging and mooring lines. In the color plate it is the geometrical design made on the sand by mooring ropes and chains that is the real subject; the boats themselves establish the scale and plane of the pattern.

Figure 60 and Color Plate 16 are two interpretations of the same subject by a painter-illustrator friend of mine. Color Plate 16 was more or less literal, although not entirely so (in fact I believe there was a previous drawing in which more factual detail was recorded). A process of simplification, strengthening, and rationalization then led to the silkscreen print based on the painting. As you can see, it is not accurate in photographic terms. Or if it is, then the painting can't be. Indeed, perhaps it shouldn't even be called by the name of the original harbor, yet despite its distortions the last picture has more of the intrinsic character of the place than the more "accurate" one. I know this particular harbor well, and from the outermost arm of the sea wall on a sunny day there is a strong impression of clean, sharp-edged whiteness, quite stark against the textured, rather rounded, hill behind. There are, in fact, houses and beach huts, roads, and trees in the background, but they have all been left out. The fact that they were there is not sufficient reason to include them, if their inclusion would, as here, clutter the clear statement

60. (Above) **Location Sketch** by Alan Jessett. A silkscreen print was made by the artist based on his painting (see Color Plate 16).

59. (Left) **Moored Boats, Ilfracombe Harbour.** This scene done in sepia ink from my sketchbook shows the pattern created by moored boats that can excite the eye of the artist.

61. Black Lion Wharf, Wapping by J.A.M. Whistler. The etching of this riverscape shows richness and texture of detail, especially in the stones, tile, and brick of the warehouses in the background.

62. (Left) **St. Ives** by Ben Nicholson. This calm, cool painting of a harbor seen through a window is given interpretive texture by the artist. (The Tate Gallery, London)

63. (Right) **On Board Ship.** One of numerous drawings from my sketchbook, this scene does not depict an actual seascape, but one exciting aspect of life on the sea.

64. (Left) **Sea Front, Weymouth.** The strong verticals of the watchtower and telephone line poles contrast strongly with the horizontal of the river.

65. (Right) **Beach Scene.** Another scene from my sketchbook shows bathers by the sea shore, another interesting subject for drawing.

66. Lobster Pots. Manmade seaside objects such
lobster pots cannot be ignored as subjects for
drawings and paintings: they can be said to be
sea-formed and sometimes resemble natural sea
phenomena.

of harbor wall and sea against the simple land mass.

Christopher Wood's painting (Figure 14, p. 25) shows that you don't necessarily have to be able to draw form and perspective realistically and accurately in order to produce a good picture. Indeed, it is the almost childlike directness of imagery, uninhibited by the need for "correct" scale and depth rendition, that gives his pictures their charm.

Whistler's etching (Figure 61) is not strictly a marine picture, but a riverscape. However, it does show what richness of texture and detail can be extracted from waterside impediments. No doubt a gray tone could have been laid to represent the general color of those warehouses, but it was clearly the subtly different textures of stone, tile, and brick that interested him, so there was no alternative but painstakingly to draw them all in.

I would like to point out that this doesn't mean that de Stael by contrast is getting away with it, skating over the surface, so to speak. He was setting out to express something quite different, and the extreme simplicity may have been the final result.

The de Stael (Figure 13, p. 24) and the Ben Nicholson (Figure 62) are both sophisticated and stylish, simplified statements, the former depending on absolute first-time directness and bold color, the latter, calm, cool, thoughtful, lovingly textured.

Figures 63 through 66 are drawings from my sketchbook, which just touch on a series of subjects which could justify a book to themselves. It would seem that until now I have ignored the fact that the seaside is often teeming with human beings and the fabrications for their amusement. I don't mean to sneer; I just find that I have run out of room and time before getting around to this other, and for me I confess slightly less interesting, aspect of the sea.

Conclusion

I would like to make it clear that I do not put forward my own drawings and paintings as ends in themselves. They merely serve to make a point or two and represent a stage in my continuing, but far from final, observations of the sea. Be influenced, if you must, by the masters; then you should be able to do much better than I have.

You have, as an amateur painter, the big advantage of not having to show professional technical expertise. I think it futile and possibly damaging for a nonprofessional painter to try above all to acquire these skills.

Basic methods and organization of materials to minimize wasted time and effort, some perspective principles, and color theory are worth learning, but concentration of effort on acquiring a facile technique is likely to be self-defeating in that what you will probably end up with is a set of superficial tricks, which get in the way of observation and expression.

A technique that fits what you have to say and how you want to say it will come as long as you don't think about it too much.

Observation, resulting in discovery, is the number one requirement of objective painting, especially important when painting the sea.

Next, perhaps, come simplicity and restraint, which do not—repeat not—exclude verve, audacity, and strength. It just means that you should try to concentrate on one aspect of a subject, ruthlessly subordinating all elements which do not contribute to the total effect.

Last, be sure that you are interested in the subject. If you are not, your boredom will be obvious in your painting. If you are interested in your subject, your creativity will show in your painting.

Bibliography

Ballinger, Harry R., *Painting Sea and Shore.* New York, Watson-Guptill Publications, 1966.

FitzGerald, Edmond J., *Marine Painting in Watercolor.* New York, Watson-Guptill Publications, 1972.

Olsen, Herb, *Painting the Marine Scene in Watercolor.* New York, Van Nostrand Reinhold, 1967.

Pellew, John C., *Oil Painting Outdoors.* New York, Watson-Guptill Publications, 1971.

Raynes, John, *Starting to Paint in Oils.* New York, Watson-Guptill Publications, 1966.

Raynes, John, *Starting to Paint with Acrylics.* New York, Watson-Guptill Publications, 1969.

Shumaker, Philip G., *Painting the Sea.* New York, Sterling Publishers, 1966.

Smart, Borlase, *Seascape Painting Step-by-Step.* New York, Watson-Guptill Publications, 1969.

Woodward, Stanley, *Marine Painting in Oil and Watercolor.* New York, Watson-Guptill Publications, 1967.

Index

Acrylics, 9, 12

Boats, 45, 93, 95, 101

Carrying frames, 19
Color, 21–34; of sea and sky, 7, 21; theory, 21
Color changes, of the sea, 7, 21, 33
Color key, in painting, 26
Color sketches, making, 29
Color spectrum, illus., 23
Colors, complementary, 21; mixing and matching, 28; primary, 21; seaside, 93, 95
Comfort, painting outdoors versus, 69, 71
Complementary colors, 21
Composition, devices, 36; objects in, 80, 85
Crustaceans, 85

De Stael, Nicholas, 26, 111; illus. by, 24
Drawing kit, 9
Duffel bag, 16

Easels, 19; illus., 13, 18, 19
Equipment, painting, 9–20
Experiences, sea, 88
Eye level. See Horizon line.

Fauna, sea, 85–92
Fish, 88
Flora, sea, 85–92
Forms, sea, 7

Hokusai, 59; illus. by, 54
Horizon line, placement of, 35

Imagination, using your, 61, 63

Jessett, Alan, illus. by, 100, 103

Kit. See Paint kits.

Man, and the sea, 93–112
Materials. See Equipment.
Mediums, choosing, 9
Monoprinting, 63
Movement, of the sea, 47–60

Nicholson, Ben, 111; illus. by, 106
Notes, taking, 56

Objects, in composition, 80, 85
Oil paints, 9, 12, 14
Outdoors, painting versus comfort, 69, 70

Paint kits, 14–16; illus., 14, 15, 16
Paintbox, 16. See also Paint kits.
Painting, interpretive, 101, 111
Painting surfaces, 12, 16
Paints, acrylic, 9, 12; oil based, 9, 12, 14; water based, 9, 12, 14
Palettes, illus., 27; layout of, 26, 28
Papers. See Painting surfaces.
Patterns, 39, 45; of waves, 56
Perspective, 45
Photos, illus., 55; use of, 33, 59
Pigments, 21–26
Pitfalls, how to avoid, 59
Pointillism, 33
Primary colors, 21

Rocks, shoreline, 61, 63

Sea, and sky, 7; color of, 7, 21–34; mobile, 47; shape of, 35–46
Seaside structures, 93; colors of, 93, 95; patterns of, 93, 95
Seaweed, 85
Seurat, Georges, 33; illus. by, 31
Shape, of the sea, 35–46
Shells, 85
Shore, 61–84
Sketches, 56; making color, 29, 56
Sky, color of sea and, 7, 21

"Statement," making a 56, 58
Study, of movement, 47; of shoreline rocks,
    61

Tone, values of, 37, 39
Turner, J. M. W., 59; illus. by, 57

View, searching for the right, 70; sub-
    aquatic, 85
Vision, selective, 95, 107

Watercolors, 9, 12, 14
Waves, 47, 56; patterns of, 56
Whistler, J. A. M., 111; illus. by 104–105
Wood, Christopher, 26, 101, 111; illus. by, 28

Edited by Juliana W. Goldman
Designed by James Craig and Robert Fillie
Set in 9 point Helvetica by Publishers Graphics, Inc.
Printed and bound in Japan by Toppan Printing Company, Ltd.